D1411288

Integrated Marketing for Colleges, Universities, and Schools

A Step-by-Step Planning Guide

By Robert A. Sevier

Vice President for Research and Marketing
Stamats Communications, Inc.

COUNCIL FOR ADVANCEMENT
AND SUPPORT OF EDUCATION

ISBN 0-89964-321-3

Printed in the United States of America

COUNCIL FOR
ADVANCEMENT
AND SUPPORT OF
EDUCATION

In 1974, the American Alumni Council (founded in 1913) and the American College Public Relations Association (founded in 1917) merged to become the Council for Advancement and Support of Education (CASE).

Today, nearly 3,000 colleges, universities, independent elementary and secondary schools, educationally related nonprofit organizations, and commercial firms in the United States, Canada, Mexico, and 34 other countries belong to CASE. This makes CASE the largest nonprofit 501(c)(3) education association in terms of institutional membership. Representing the member institutions in CASE are more than 15,000 individual professionals in institutional advancement.

Nonprofit education-related organizations such as hospitals, museums, libraries, cultural or performing arts groups, public radio and television stations, or foundations established for public elementary and secondary schools may affiliate with CASE as Educational Associates. Commercial firms that serve the education field may affiliate as Supplier and Consultant Affiliates.

The purposes of the Council for Advancement and Support of Education (CASE) are to develop and foster sound relationships between member educational institutions and their constituencies; to provide training programs, products, and services in the areas of alumni relations, communications, and philanthropy; to promote diversity within these professions; and to provide a strong force for the advancement and support of education worldwide.

CASE offers books, videotapes, and focus issues of its award-winning monthly magazine, CURRENTS, to professionals in institutional advancement. The books cover topics in alumni relations, communications, fund raising, management, and student recruitment. For a copy of the catalog, RESOURCES, or for more information about CASE programs and services, call (202) 328-5900.

Copyeditors: Ellen Ryan, Nancy Raley, and Shannon Joyce
Research: Barbara Perkins
Design and Production: Fletcher Design

Council for Advancement and Support of Education
1307 New York Ave., NW
Suite 1000
Washington, DC 20005-4701

Table of Contents

Author's Note

I couldn't have written this book without the contributions of the countless colleagues and clients, who, over the years, became friends. And while it is dangerous to list people because the likelihood is high that I will overlook someone, there are simply some people who must be mentioned. First, Stewart Dyke, my first real boss and mentor. There is seldom a day that goes by that I don't remember something he taught me. Next, Joe Cope, Bob Smith, Jeannie Morelock, Bob Johnson, and Daryl Gilley; five people who don't know each other but who have all impacted my life and my work. I would love to have all of you over for dinner at the same time. And there are others: Sharon Saunders, Darrell Marks, John Weems, LaRose Spooner, Steve Briggs, and Bonnie Black who deserve mention. For the hundreds of conversations, e-mail messages, shared books and articles, faxes, telephone calls; for the advice and insight, but most of all, for the encouragement and friendship, I am in your debt.

There are a handful of others a bit closer to home whom I must acknowledge. Guy Wendler and Peter Stamats; thank you for encouraging me in this undertaking. For Tom Jackson and Marilyn Osweiler, two of the most honorable people I know and people whom I am lucky to count as friends. And for those who work closest with me: Becky, Suzanne, Steve, Toni, Lorna, Sally, Dennis, Lisa, and Annette. Thanks for keeping me pointed in the right direction.

And finally, I want to thank my Mom and Dad. My Dad was a lover of books and words and I know that he would have been proud of this effort. And I know that my Mom is. Thanks also to my wonderful and patient son, Andy. "Hey bud, the book's done. Let's play." And finally, I would like to thank Pat, my wife. She is my best friend, my greatest adviser, and the most generous person I know. Without her support, this book, and all my successes, both professional and personal, simply would not have happened.

Introduction

I well remember the meeting. The president of a good-sized college in the Midwest was huddled with his board on a snowy afternoon. The institution was in trouble. Enrollment was down, and the college had just gone through a round of staff layoffs. The closing of one, perhaps two, academic departments was planned for early spring. The budget was deeply in the red, and the president had asked me to help the college explore its options.

The conversation was surprisingly frank . . . and pointed. Some board members wanted to fire the director of admissions. Others seemed convinced that the faculty needed to work harder. When the president left the room for a short period, one board member openly criticized his leadership. "He has no vision," she said.

As the afternoon wore on, the conversation began to take a new tack. "What we need," said one board member, "is a marketing plan."

"Yes," said another, "we need to advertise. We need to get the word out."

Before adjourning, the board voted to fund a marketing campaign. "We need to show the campus that we are moving forward," said the board chair.

I left campus that evening wondering if marketing could really help that institution.

Thinking back, I am convinced that my deep fascination for higher education marketing—and the genesis for this book—began on that cold afternoon.

A road well traveled

Since that day, I have worked with hundreds of colleges and universities throughout the country. Over the years I have become more convinced than ever that, yes, marketing could have helped that institution—and furthermore, that the majority of America's colleges, universities, and schools would benefit from a comprehensive marketing plan.

Of course, I don't mean the misdirected marketing campaign proposed by that well-intentioned board member. Rather, I mean a comprehensive approach to marketing that is founded on the following definition:

> **Marketing is the analysis, planning, implementation, and control of carefully formulated programs designed to bring about voluntary exchanges of values with target markets for the purpose of achieving organizational objectives.**

A marketing planning process is one that is built on solid research . . .

– that includes not only promotion strategies but product, price, and place strategies as well
– that seeks to establish vital exchange relationships with key target audiences
– that is designed to achieve specific organizational objectives: objectives outlined in the college or university's mission, vision, and strategic plan

This is the type of marketing that would have helped that institution. These days it is called *integrated marketing*.

But why this book?

Over the years, as I read books and articles on marketing and attended seminars and symposia, I came to four conclusions.

First, very little of the current literature on higher education marketing is really about colleges, universities, and schools. Most of it is a rehash of marketing principles and ideas from the corporate world. Useful at times, but a bit ill-fitting.

Second, much of what passes as marketing is really promotion. There seems to be an underlying sense that many problems could be solved by simply turning up the volume a bit—getting the message out to more people.

Third, almost none of the information on marketing has a true institution-wide focus. Most of it addresses marketing from a single perspective: public relations, recruiting, or fund-raising—it is not integrated marketing.

And finally, none of the material addresses planning in an academic environment, an environment in which the decision-making process is often more important than the quality and utility of the decision itself.

I wrote this book to help address these problems.

A step-by-step approach to marketing

The marketing planning process outlined here is different, and, I hope, important, for a number of reasons.

First, this book uses education as its sole reference point. The steps and processes reflect the very real opportunities and constraints found on campuses. The planning process outlined here recognizes how colleges think and act and sometimes don't act. This book was written specifically for colleges, universities, and schools, not radio stations or manufacturers. Although this book is written more for higher education, private primary and secondary schools can also benefit.

Second, this book is decidedly practical. It includes a great number of "how-to" lists, and steps to follow. It is not intended for the marketing purist, who already has plenty of sources, but for the group or individual who must write and implement a marketing plan.

Third, this book recognizes that a college, university, or school's marketing plan must be consistent with its mission and vision. The planning process outlined here stresses the need for strong, declarative leadership—and shows that marketing is best seen as an extension of, not a replacement for, strategic planning.

Fourth, this marketing planning process is designed for everyone from the novice to the experienced marketer and is highly interactive yet sequential. It moves through three distinct stages:

1. Building the foundation
2. Writing the plan
3. Execution and evaluation

Next, unlike many marketing texts, this book emphasizes the need for evaluation: of the marketing plan, of individual marketing activities, and of the process itself.

Finally, unlike the majority of books on marketing that stress the written plan, this book recognizes that it is not the plan that is important but the planning process. My goal is to help you develop an ongoing process that recognizes, even anticipates, opportunities and obstacles in a fluid and dynamic marketplace.

Organization

The book is organized into three broad sections. The first section makes the case for marketing. Chapter 1 explores the following five challenges and explains how they will affect colleges and universities:

1. The changing demographics of college students
2. Cost to attend and the tuition gap between publics and privates
3. The rise of publics, including two-year institutions, as major players
4. The greater involvement of states in managing their public institutions
5. Increased competition for the donated dollar

Chapter 2 suggests that higher education's major challenges are compounded by administrators' inability or reluctance to make tough decisions in a timely fashion. It then outlines the role that institutional mission, vision, and leadership play in the marketing planning process.

Chapter 3 presents an expanded definition of marketing that focuses on exchange relationships—the need for both target audiences and institutions to be satisfied through the process. Chapter 3 also details the four Ps of marketing: product, price, place, and promotion.

Chapter 4 explores the differences between qualitative and quantitative research and outlines the need for trend data. Chapter 4 also addresses issues relating to sampling and validity, then reviews the steps for undertaking a research project: creating the agenda, designing the methodology, designing the instrument and questions, drawing the sample, completing the study, inputting and analyzing the data, and presenting the results. The chapter concludes with a list of sources for inexpensive secondary research.

Chapter 5 makes the case that institutional image is your most important asset. It shows how strong images are the foundation for effective student recruiting and fund raising.

Chapter 6 introduces segmentation, an extremely useful yet underutilized marketing tool. Geographic, demographic, psychographic, and behavioral segmentation strategies are crucial for educational institutions to raise dollars and recruit students more effectively.

Section II, on the planning process itself, is the heart of the book. The three chapters in this section (outlined in Table I-1) are designed to move you sequentially through the process.

Chapter 7 addresses the need to empower the marketing planning process, clarify your purpose, and designate a champion. This chapter also discusses who should be on the marketing team and how to build the team, and it defines planning relationships and terminology.

Chapter 8 outlines the seven steps to writing the plan, including undertaking a situational analysis, clarifying marketing goals and target audiences, writing a marketing action plan, budgeting, and debugging the plan.

The last chapter in this section is designed to help you evaluate not only your plan but the overall process.

The third and final section will help you troubleshoot and improve the effectiveness of both your plan and the process so they can better meet your institution's needs and expectations now and in the future.

The book closes with a comprehensive list of secondary research sources; a compilation of marketing, research, and higher education World Wide Web sites; and one of the most exhaustive higher education marketing bibliographies ever assembled.

At the very time that the need for strong leadership in higher education has reached new levels of urgency, academic management is in chains. Indeed, the whole subject of administration in higher education is befuddled by rusty myths and hoary options about authority, management, and leadership.

Section I
Why Marketing, Why Now?

1

Why Marketing, Why Now?

Educational institutions face an unprecedented and sometimes bewildering array of challenges to their growth and prosperity. Founding missions, to some minds, seem increasingly ill-suited for the demands of today's marketplace. Budgets are excruciatingly tight while voices and programs clamor for financial support. Governance is contested at virtually every turn. Increased oversight often leads to unreasonable demands for accountability. A paralyzed decision-making process makes progress difficult, tenuous, and overly politicized. And the recruiting and fund-raising marketplace is very competitive, sometimes even hostile.

Five megatrends

This array of problems facing higher education is not new. What is new is the convergence of five megatrends that alone or together could dramatically affect institutions' ability to exert their own will in the marketplace:

1. The changing demographics of college students
2. Cost to attend and the tuition gap between publics and privates
3. The rise of publics, including two-year institutions, as major players in recruiting and fund raising

4. Greater involvement of states in managing their public institutions
5. Increased competition for the donated dollar

Megatrend No. 1: Changing demographics

There is no magic in demography, no surprises. Demographic projections, particularly those of national scope, are usually forthright, easily documented, and widely accepted. Although the data are usually straightforward, sometimes an understanding of their impact is not.

Table 1-1 shows an important shift in the projected ethnic composition of the

Table 1-1.

Population by Race and Hispanic Origin: 1990-2050 [In thousands. As of July 1. Resident population]

| Year | Total | Race | | | | Hispanic Origin[3] | Not of Hispanic Origin | | | |
		White	Black	American Indian[1]	Asian[2]		White	Black	American Indian[1]	Asian[2]
ESTIMATE										
1990	249,402	209,180	30,599	2,073	7,550	22,549	188,601	29,374	1,802	7,076
PROJECTIONS										
Middle Series										
1995	262,820	218,078	33,144	2,241	9,357	26,936	193,566	31,598	1,931	8,788
2000	274,634	225,532	35,454	2,402	11,245	31,366	197,061	33,568	2,054	10,584
2005	285,981	232,463	37,734	2,572	13,212	36,057	199,802	35,485	2,183	12,454
2010	297,716	239,588	40,109	2,754	15,265	41,139	202,390	37,466	2,320	14,402
2020	322,742	254,887	45,075	3,129	19,651	52,652	207,393	41,538	2,601	18,557
2030	346,899	269,046	50,001	3,515	24,337	65,570	209,998	45,448	2,891	22,993
2040	369,980	281,720	55,094	3,932	29,235	80,164	209,621	49,379	3,203	27,614
2050	393,931	294,615	60,592	4,371	34,352	96,508	207,901	53,555	3,534	32,432
Lowest Series										
2050	282,524	213,782	44,477	3,383	20,882	62,230	157,701	40,118	2,793	19,683
Highest Series										
2050	518,903	381,505	81,815	5,384	50,199	133,106	262,140	71,863	4,295	47,498

[1]American Indian represents American Indian, Eskimo, and Aleut.
[2]Asian represents Asian and Pacific Isalander.
[3]Persons of Hispanic origin may be of any race. The information on the total and Hispanic population shown in this report was collected in the 50 States and the District of Columbia and, therefore, does not include residents of Puerto Rico.
Source: U.S. Department of Commerce, Economics and Statistics Administration, Bureau of the Census, 1996.

U.S. population over the next 50 years. From a demographic perspective, there will be little growth, and even some decline, in the Caucasian population. However, we will see strong growth among Hispanics and Asians and a very slight growth among African Americans. There will be little real growth in the number of Native Americans during this time.

Raw census numbers tell part of the story, but percentages tell more. By 2050, Hispanics will compose nearly 25 percent of our population—up from 10 percent in 1997. Asians, meanwhile, will increase as a percentage of our population from 3.5 percent in 1997 to 8.2 percent in 2050. However, the percentage of Caucasians will drop from 73.3 percent to 52.8. Some demographers estimate that as an ethnic group, Caucasians will slip into minority status about the year 2060. At that time the United States will have more nonwhites than whites.

But what do such demographic shifts mean? Obviously, in the immediate and foreseeable future, college students are much more likely to be of color than ever before. This issue is both complex and emotionally charged: Whereas these shifts present students of color with the opportunity for unparalleled access to higher education, there is great concern about how this shift will affect the academy.

One clear impact will be economic. A sad reality of our society is that nonwhite populations simply do not, on average, have the financial resources of white populations. Current data show that nonwhite students are much less likely to be able to afford full or significant portions of their tuition; they are more likely to be on financial aid. Even as administrators and faculty look forward to meeting these students' educational needs, they have serious concerns about who will be paying the bills.

The second impact will be on higher education's character and composition. Nonwhite students are less likely to be residential and to attend school full-time, and are more likely to require extensive support services. They are more likely to attend public two- and four-year institutions rather than private ones. For colleges and universities dependent on white, residential students, the impact of this shift will be significant and ongoing.

Along with these demographic shifts will be some attitudinal shifts. Students of today, and tomorrow, are

- Somewhat more conservative than previous generations of students
- Likely to be less interested in the pure liberal arts
- Very program- and outcomes-oriented
- More practical
- More likely to include convenience and access in defining academic quality

Embedded in these demographic shifts is a subtle nuance. We also know that tomorrow's college students are likely to be older and somewhat more likely to arrive on campus with a GED rather than a traditional diploma.

But those aren't our students

Of course, you might be trying to let yourself off the demographic hook by saying, "We don't recruit these kinds of students—this doesn't apply to me or my institution." In a very narrow sense this may be true. But keep in mind one more thought: The full-time, traditional-age, residential student with better-than-average academics and some ability to pay will be the minority for the foreseeable future. Not only will the number of these students decline, but the need for institutions to recruit these students will grow. In short, these students will be the most sought-after cohort in higher education. Institutions with deep pockets, great name recognition, or both will win at recruiting them; institutions with little recognition or money for non-loan-based aid will face extremely challenging times.

> **The full-time, traditional age, residential student with better-than-average academics and some ability to pay will be the minority of the future.**

Students and their baggage

Tomorrow's students are also much more likely to arrive on campus with unreasonable expectations, or what one sociologist terms "a galloping psychology of entitlement." More and more students believe that you owe them an on-time education even though they will have trouble making decisions, keeping commitments, and being responsible for their actions. I well remember one president reminding me, "Tomorrow's students will be much like their parents, and their parents are people like us."

There is one final characteristic that must be mentioned—perhaps the most troubling one of all. Many of tomorrow's students will arrive on your campus with significant, often long-term physical and emotional health problems. They will come to your institution from broken or abusive homes. They will have been exposed to AIDS. They will be using more drugs, prescribed and illegal, than any previous generation of college students. And alcoholism and binge drinking will continue to be a problem.

To meet such needs, colleges and universities must be prepared to invest significant resources (time, money, and talent) in assessment, counseling, health services, and, unfortunately, campus security.

The impact on colleges and universities

These trends will affect higher education in two ways. First, there is little debate that they will heighten the already significant stresses on recruiting, financial aid, and student services.

The second impact is more subtle and long-term: There is increasing evidence that tomorrow's students will not make especially good alumni. Because they are less likely to be residential and to partake in traditional campus-life activities—and much more likely to drop in and out, attend part-time, and transfer from one institution to another—they are not as inclined to feel strong loyalty to a single institution.

In 1995, according to Stamats Communications, Inc. research, some 27 percent of all donated dollars came directly from alumni. Another significant portion came from alumni via the corporations and foundations where they work. Alumni loyalty plays a tremendous role in fund raising. That's why campuses must begin active assessment of young alumni needs.

Megatrend No. 2: Cost to attend and tuition gap between publics and privates

The second megatrend is economic, not demographic. It has six dimensions:

1. Cost to attend college
2. Widening tuition gap between publics and privates
3. Falling family contribution
4. Tuition discounting
5. Shifting financial-aid patterns
6. Debt load of college graduates

> "There is increasing evidence that tomorrow's students will not make especially good alumni."

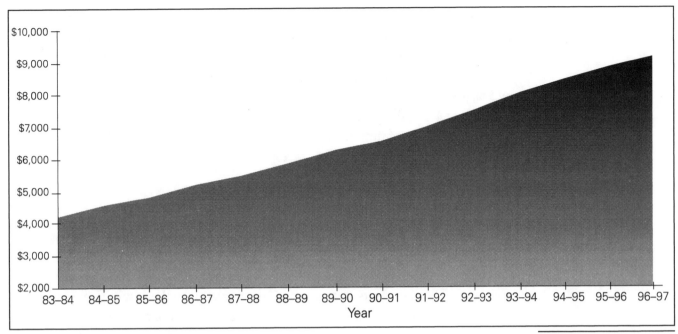

Figure 1-1.
Average Undergraduate Tuition, Fees, Room and Board at All U.S. Colleges and Universities

Source: U.S. Department of Education, National Center for Educational Statistics, *Digest of Educational Statistics*, 1997, Table 312.

Figure 1-2.
Increase in the Cost of Selected Goods and Services: 1982-1992

Source: Bureau of Labor Statistics, Consumer Price Index, Personal Consumption Expenditure Price Indices, 1996.

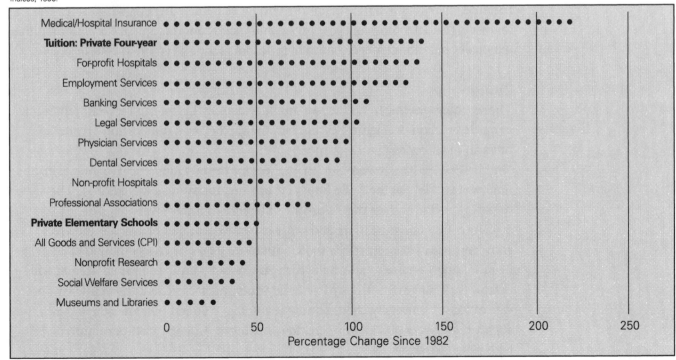

College cost

By any measure, attending college is expensive. The literature, both popular and professional, is replete with stories of soaring tuition costs that usually outpace the rate of inflation and the growth of the consumer price index (CPI), in some cases by a factor of two to one.

Figure 1-1 and Figure 1-2 show this rate of increase dramatically. The first shows a 14-year overview of tuition, room, and board charges at all U.S. colleges and universities. The second shows this same increase juxtaposed against the rate of increase for other goods and services in the U.S. economy.

The perception of college cost

The reality of college cost is bad enough. But many constituents perceive college costs as even higher than they really are. Studies by the American Council on Education, the National Association of College Admissions Counselors, and other associations indicate that both students and parents often overestimate the cost of going to college.

Feeding this angst is the annual media blitz that accompanies the decision by colleges to raise their tuition each year. From *Newsweek* to *USA Today* to the *Washington Monthly*, we see such headlines as these:

- $1,000 a Week—The Scary Cost of College
- How Colleges Are Gouging U
- Middle Class Sees Diploma in Doubt
- Tuition Races Ahead of Inflation—Again
- Highbrow Robbery

> "There is little doubt that more and more families believe, without really knowing, that attending college is not within their economic reach."

Certainly this somewhat alarmist presentation of college cost affects the rate at which high school students go on to college. And though the exact impact is difficult to measure, there is little doubt that more and more families believe, without really knowing, that attending college is not within their economic reach. Keep in mind that nationally, only about 50 percent of high school graduates go on to college.

Tuition gap

The second economic trend focuses on the widening tuition gap between public and private education. As Figure 1-3 suggests, the gap between publics and privates is often an order of magnitude or more.

In 1995-96, the average tuition and fees for the 604 four-year U.S. public institutions was $6,325. For the 1,586 four-year privates, the average was $17,851. The tuition gap—the average public/private difference in price—was $11,526.

As colleges become more and more expensive, families of average and even above-average means, especially those with more than one college-bound child, will be increasingly unable to afford the cost. Simple but painful economic realities will narrow their range of options. Where they once might have sent their child to a private college or university, they are now beginning to attend publics. Where they once attended four-year publics, they are now looking at two-year institutions, perhaps with plans to transfer.

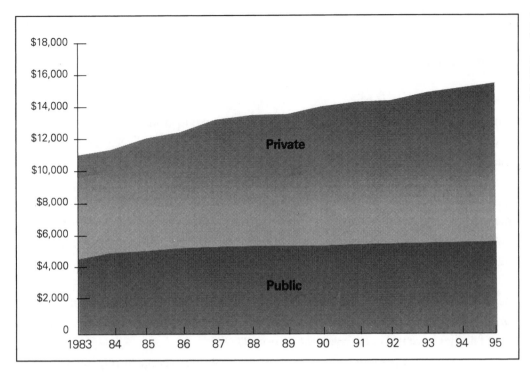

Figure 1-3.
Ten-Year Cost to Attend College: Publics vs. Privates
Source:Stamats Communications, Inc.

Falling family income

Because of the very real evidence that family and disposable income will continue to slide well into the next century, we cannot expect college costs to become more manageable. Even as a small group of middle-class families is becoming more affluent—especially those with two wage earners—a much larger group is losing ground. By many estimates, we are seeing a squeeze of the middle class. This is especially compounded by an increasing number of single-parent families. A colleague in financial aid at a Pacific Northwest college told me recently that she is not worried about the ability of affluent families to afford college and even less worried about the institution's ability to help poor students. "What greatly concerns me," she said, "is our ability, and the interest of either the state or the federal government, to meet the financial aid needs of middle-class families. They are being pushed out of higher education."

Private higher education

The high cost to attend will hurt all colleges and universities, but especially private ones. The tuition gap offers a long-term opportunity for publics. Unless private colleges and universities are able to offer significant financial aid, families that traditionally sent their sons and daughters to private institutions will, in the future, be much more likely to choose public ones.

Family savings rates

This concern about college cost and the tuition gap is especially acute when a family has not saved significant dollars for children's education. Though the quantifiable

> **Unless private colleges and universities are able to offer significant financial aid, families will be more likely to choose public ones.**

data are sketchy, there is every reason to believe that the rate at which families save for college has stagnated. Fewer are saving enough money even to pay a significant portion of tuition bills.

Choosing on the basis of cost

Families that have saved little will find their educational options severely constricted. They will be much be more inclined in the future to choose a college based not on quality or program but on cost.

An interesting study in an *American Demographics* article by Tibbett Spear makes this point clearly. The magazine noted that in 1994, the average family that intended to send a son or daughter to a private institution estimated that the total cost of attending for four years was $50,000. By the time the student was a junior in high school, though, that same family had saved less than $6,000 toward college.

A 1997 study by Stamats adds a new dimension to our discussion of family savings rates. We found that while the average family has saved about $5,700 for college, some 78 percent of the respondents had saved far less. Not only is the average low, but most families have not even saved that amount.

These data are troubling for three reasons. First, the average family has saved so little. Second, the family has seriously underestimated the cost of a private college. And third, the family has underestimated, by about 20 percent, how long it takes the average student to graduate from college. Too many families have saved too little for a college education that is more expensive than they estimate, and they will be paying tuition, room, and board for a longer period than they think.

Tuition discounting

Another potentially destructive economic trend is tuition discounting: the amount, expressed as a percentage of the total tuition cost, that a college or university discounts tuition by awarding institutional financial aid. For example, let's assume that a college charges $10,000 a year and recruits a class of 500 students. The tuition revenue, if everyone paid full tuition, would be $5 million. However, the college spends $1 million of its operating budget on financial aid. Therefore, the net tuition revenue is actually $4 million. The college has discounted tuition 20 percent. For all practical purposes, its tuition is really $8,000 a year. It has discounted its tuition, but it has not lowered its costs to educate a student.

Table 1-2 indicates the rise in tuition discount rates for public and private four-year institutions in 1994 and 1995.

This idea is not new; colleges and universities have been discounting tuition since their inception. However, the degree of discounting has taken an alarming turn: More institutions are discounting tuition to a much higher degree. A number of private institutions have tuition discount rates of 35 percent and higher. This places a tremendous burden on their budgets. Once tuition discounting begins, it is very difficult to end.

Excessive discounting is poor financial policy under the best of circumstances.

Table 1-2.
Rise in Percentage of Tuition Discount Rates

Year and Type of Institution	Discount Rate
Public/1994	19.6
Public/1995	20.1
Private/1994	24.7
Private/1995	25.6

However, it is especially problematic when the size of the freshman class is static. If your classes are shrinking, tuition discounting may put your institution in a financial straitjacket from which it may never escape.

Shifting financial aid patterns

Even as families struggle to keep up with rising tuition, room, and board costs, we have seen a dramatic shift in the ratio of grants to loans in the typical financial aid package. As the graph in Figure 1-4 indicates, in 1975 the typical package was about 60 percent grants and about 20 percent loans. Two decades later, however, the typical aid package was 20 percent grants and 60 percent loans. As a result, more students are graduating with more debt—often very significant debt.

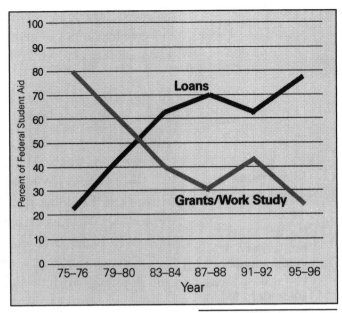

Figure 1-4.
Change in Composition of Typical Financial Aid Package, 1975 through 1995

Source: College Board, *Trends in Student Aid: 1986–1996*, Table 1 and Appendix Table A.

Graduate debt load

The final economic trend concerns the debt load of college graduates. Tomorrow's graduates of both public and private campuses are facing an increasing level of college debt.

In 1995, the median debt for all students at graduation was $10,150. There is considerable evidence that the debt for students attending a private institution is much higher—some say nearly double the median. Students attending a public institution are likely to owe less. See Table 1-3.

Although this debt is troublesome for several reasons, one in particular stands out: Students who are interested in social work, education, and even the ministry are looking at their potential debt and opting for majors and careers that are more lucrative. Thus debt penalizes not just students but society.

The September 1997 *Postsecondary Education Opportunity* report highlights the impact of college debt on students and graduates. We know from experience that high debt rate negatively affects time to degree, graduation rate, career choices after graduation, and even when to marry and how many children to have. And alumni directors are keenly aware of another impact of college debt. As long as a graduate is paying off loans, he or she is unlikely to think positively about donating money to the institution.

One final comment about graduate debt load. A couple of years ago I had a chance to meet with the president of a top private college in Massachusetts. He was relishing its ability to run a budget surplus of $1.3 million each year. Earlier that day I had learned from the financial aid office that graduates owed, on average, $7,300 in loans. I also knew that the college graduated about 170 seniors each year. I asked the president if he was aware that the amount of his budget surplus was strikingly similar to the amount owed by his graduating class (170 students times $7,000 per student

Table 1-3.
Graduate Debt Load

Year	Percentage with Debt	Median Debt
1977	34.0	$ 2,000
1980	34.9	$ 2,500
1984	44.8	$ 5,000
1986	50.1	$ 4,800
1990	45.0	$ 7,000
1994	53.3	$ 9,100
1995	59.1	$10,150

equals $1,241,000). He said there was no relationship between the budget surplus and the debt load of his students. "Good financial management on our part," he said, "and not good financial management on theirs."

Megatrend No. 3: The impact of publics, including two-year institutions, as major players in recruiting and fund raising

All things being equal, the road ahead for public colleges and universities will be somewhat less troubled than for private ones—for a number of reasons.

First is the perception and reality of cost. Almost universally, students and parents believe that public institutions are less expensive, sometimes significantly so, than private ones. Without even investigating the matter, many families automatically rule out private higher education.

Second, tomorrow's college students are much more likely to be older, of color, and attending part-time. Public institutions, particularly two-year colleges, have established a strong track record of accommodating the unique and disparate needs of this diverse clientele.

Third, there is the issue of quality. Dick Moll, in *The Public Ivys*, was one of the first to make the case that some public institutions are doing an outstanding job of demonstrating solid quality at a reasonable price. Unfortunately for the privates, this is occurring just when privates are having a tough time justifying their higher cost. As the marketplace has been demonstrating, it is hard for private institutions to position themselves against lower-cost public ones that consistently demonstrate high quality—and more and more are.

Fourth, publics are much more likely to attract huge affinity groups—thousands of students who never really considered a private institution. Each year, for example, some 6,000 young Buckeyes decide that their immediate future rests with Ohio State. In many cases, these students have assumed since middle school or even younger that they would attend OSU. Whether it is the scarlet and gray of Ohio State, the yellow and green of Oregon, or even the red and white of Maryland, such large public institutions have a strong following due in large part to their tradition of sports. For students who decide early in life that they will attend a particular institution, others have to work very hard to be considered seriously.

Fifth, publics are, by definition, public. This is a tremendous safety net. Though they may change and evolve, very few are in danger of actually failing. States invest millions, even billions of dollars and enormous prestige in their higher education systems each year, and it is always much easier to keep supporting them than to face the political and economic fallout of trying to close one down.

Next is the issue of size. Not only are publics generally larger, enrolling more students and having larger budgets, but they have the potential for tremendous alumni networks. The University of Minnesota system, for example, has 350,000 living alumni.

Finally, public institutions are improving at promoting themselves. Publics have always enjoyed the high visibility of their athletic teams. Now the quality of their

> "Public institutions are getting much better at telling their story to audiences that are increasingly interested in hearing it."

advertising and recruiting materials has never been higher. Public institutions are getting much better at telling their story to audiences that are increasingly interested in hearing it.

When I think about the rise of public institutions in the marketplace, I am often reminded of the quote attributed to Admiral Isoruku Yamamoto just after he learned that the Japanese Imperial Navy had bombed Pearl Harbor: "I fear," he said, "that we have woken a great sleeping giant and filled that giant with a terrible resolve." Today's giants are public colleges and universities, and as they awake, they will cast an enormous shadow across higher education.

Megatrend No. 4: The greater involvement of states in managing their public institutions

The future will not be completely rosy for public institutions. In fact, from a funding and governance perspective, public four-year and, to a lesser degree, two-year institutions will be in for a stressful time. Most of this stress will emanate from a single reality—citizen reluctance to keep funding higher education without a clearer sense of where these dollars are going. One president calls this "taxpayer cynicism" and seems to resent taxpayers' intrusion into college affairs. Whether cynical or not, taxpayers have a right to know that their dollars are being used wisely and they are becoming more effective in exercising this right.

> **The future will not be completely rosy for public institutions.**

Though many of the nuances of this taxpayer "revolt" have yet to be played out, we can expect the following five actions and reactions:

1. More direct oversight from legislatures, political appointees, and governors
2. More centralized decision-making from coordinating commissions
3. Less duplication of programs, with duplication determined not by campuses but by state agencies
4. A declining contribution of state dollars
5. More dependence of public institutions on tuition and fees

The first three trends portend a decline in institutional autonomy, decision-making, and governance. The remaining two will help fuel the interest of public institutions in recruiting and fund raising and increase the already frantic competition between publics and privates.

Naturally, there will be a direct relationship between dwindling tax dollars and an institution's interest in aggressive recruiting and marketing strategies. Thomas Wallace, writing in *Change*, sums up the situation. In his searing article, "Public Higher Education Finance: The Dinosaur Age Persists," he describes "the Big Myth"—the belief by public institution administrators and faculty that as soon as the economy improves, state legislatures will invest enormous sums of tax dollars in higher education. Those days, he says, are over.

Megatrend No. 5: Increased competition for the donated dollar

This final megatrend has two dimensions: the greater competition for gifts, and the shift from private colleges and universities receiving the lion's share of corporate gifts to public institutions receiving them.

If it seems that everyone is fund raising, it's because everyone is. According to the *Chronicle of Philanthropy*, in 1995 there were 27,900 new charities, and the non-profit sector has expanded four times faster than the economy in each of the last 25 years. Nonprofits account for nearly $1 trillion in assets—that's six percent of the GNP—and employ one out of every 18 workers. Nonprofits hire cultivators, demographers, and prospect researchers. They analyze databases and zip codes and giving patterns. They hold dinners and telethons and sweepstakes. And they rake in billions and billions of dollars.

Too often, solicitations from colleges and universities are lost in the shuffle. In fact, I asked a friend who graduated from Stanford and lives on the West Coast to keep a year-long tally of how many times he was contacted by telephone and mail for donations. After 300 he quit counting. Asked if Stanford had been in touch, he said, "How should I know? I couldn't keep track of it all."

Another friend, in the throes of his first big capital campaign, called one night to talk about a gift that he had been cultivating. "We had it in the bag," he said, "but then we lost it. A museum got there before we could sign them."

The competition for donated dollars has a curious twist that again shows how public institutions are making their mark. In 1956-57, private two- and four-year institutions received 88 percent of each corporate donated dollar. Forty years later, that number had slipped to 55 percent. There is every indication that the percentage given to private higher education will continue to slide. See Figure 1-5.

The tiering of America's colleges and universities

It is hard to predict how these megatrends will affect individual colleges and universities. However, there is some evidence, largely anecdotal at this point, that institutions will find themselves arranged in four tiers. The first tier will contain a relatively small number of public and private institutions that will flourish. Their destinies are largely secure. They are well-funded and well-known, with supportive, powerful, and often very vocal alumni. Public and private multiversities such as Penn State and the University of Southern California, research institutions such as Johns Hopkins University and MIT, large privates such as Vanderbilt, and smaller privates like Brown and Grinnell are in this first tier.

The second tier contains a great number of institutions, both public and private, that will survive and may even flourish if managed adroitly and aggressively. The quality of their future will relate directly to the quality of their leadership.

The third tier contains institutions at risk: a smaller number, largely but not all private, that will face tremendous challenges. Some of these will move up to the second tier. Some will move down to the fourth tier. But most will remain in the third tier, and their future will be hesitant and embattled.

The final tier, composed largely of privates, contains institutions that will fail. Their small size, often under 800 students, and limited endowment will hinder their

---

Figure 1-5.
Private-Public Share Corporate Giving, 1956–57 and 1992–93

Source: *Voluntary Support of Education 1996* and *Voluntary Support of America's Colleges and Universities 1956–57,* Council for Aid to Education. Reprinted with permission.

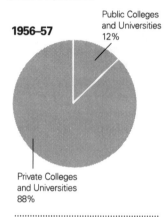

1956–57

Public Colleges and Universities 12%

Private Colleges and Universities 88%

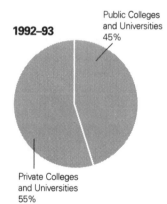

1992–93

Public Colleges and Universities 45%

Private Colleges and Universities 55%

Quick Glance

"At Risk" Characteristics

So what characteristics describe "at risk" institutions? In *Surviving the Eighties*, Lewis Mayhew developed an initial list of characteristics that describe them. While the title of the book is somewhat dated, its insights are not. Over the years I have expanded his original list to include the following:

- Lack of aggressive, knowledgeable leadership
- Frequent administrative or faculty turnover
- Loss of institutional focus
- Weak or inaccurate image
- Diminished support from its founding/nurturing public
- High operation costs compared to cohort
- Overdependency on tuition and tuition increases
- Increased institutional debt
- Small or decreasing endowment or tapping endowment to meet operating expenses
- Deferred maintenance
- Low freshman-to-sophomore retention rates
- Low graduation rates
- Difficulties in student recruiting
  - Fewer students in primary market
  - Fewer full- and fuller-pay students
  - Greater dependency on financial aid
  - Abnormally high or low amounts spent to recruit a student
- Difficulties in fund raising
  - Increased competition
  - History of small or unsuccessful capital campaigns
  - Increased competition for gifts that were historically theirs
  - Small percentage of active donors, especially alumni and trustees
  - Abnormally high cost to raise a dollar
- Poor morale
- Inflexible, bloated, or moribund curriculum that is controlled by faculty
- Lengthened time to graduate
- Faculty militancy or apathy
- Increased use of part-time faculty

ability to manage internal conflicts and marketplace challenges. They simply will not have the budgets, resources, and external support they need to survive. By some estimates, eight to 10 percent of the nation's colleges are in this bottom tier, and unfortunately colleges that the *1997 HEP Directory* notes as closed include Phillips College of Mobile, Alaska Junior College, Baptist Christian College, Spencer College, Vennard College, and Northeast Institute of Education. The odds are high that this list will grow much longer in the years to come.

Colleges and universities respond

Administrators, particularly those from third- and fourth-tier institutions, are responding to these five megatrends in a variety of ways. Some, like one small Kansas college, are in denial. They refuse to admit the magnitude of these challenges—blindly, but not blissfully, following a path chosen a century before. Others, such as a small, directionless church-related college in Illinois, hunker down, waiting for the ill winds to pass by. They know things aren't right, but they refuse to face the challenges that threaten them.

Some, like a public regional institution in California, latch on to the newest management fad with the zeal of a new convert. They hold meetings, build teams, and revise policies and procedures. They manage by bestseller and sing the praises of the latest management fad until the next quick fix makes the conference and workshop circuit.

Others, like one four-year public in Michigan, react and react again. They quickly change programs, policies, and even chief administrators, believing that their willingness to react will be enough.

There is one final group of colleges and universities—a small but growing one. Perhaps borrowing a page from a text used by their business faculty, these administrators have initiated a carefully designed planning process. They have begun to assess their marketplace carefully and systematically, rank their target audiences, and develop realistic, well-funded marketing goals. They have chosen to respond to current and coming challenges with a new or renewed commitment to visionary leadership and marketing.

2

Vision and Leadership in a New Era of Planning

A new era for planning

We are entering a new era for planning in higher education. In the first era, we planned in response to plenty. This time, we plan in response to scarcity. One college president noted that higher education has moved from the Golden Age to the Age of Survival.

In the first chapter of this book I outlined some of the significant challenges facing higher education, including

- The changing demographics of college students
- Cost to attend and the tuition gap between publics and privates
- The rise of publics, including two-year institutions, as major players
- The greater involvement of states in managing their public institutions
- Increased competition for the donated dollar

Exacerbating these challenges is a crisis in leadership: Too many colleges and universities are unable to develop effective and timely solutions. At a time when good decisions are needed most, institutions' ability to make them is at an all-time low. The ability of individual colleges and universities to navigate a safe course in increasingly treacherous seas has been severely hindered by what George Keller, in *Academic Strategy*, calls a stalemate in the exercise of power on the American campus: "At the very time that the need for strong leadership in higher education has reached new levels of urgency, academic management is in chains. Indeed, the whole subject of administration in higher education is befuddled and bound by rusty myths and hoary options about authority, management, and leadership."

Looking over our shoulders

The challenges facing America's colleges and universities are far more complex than changing demographics, smaller budgets, and more competition for donations and students. These problems are significant, but higher education has always had problems and surely always will. What is more significant is our inability to respond effectively.

In one of my favorite quotes, Michael Cohen and James March write in a 1972 issue of *Administrative Science Quarterly*:

> The American college or university is a prototypic organization anarchy. It does not know what it is doing. Its goals are either vague or in dispute. Its technology is familiar but not understood. Its major participants wander in and out of the organization. These factors do not make a university a bad organization or a disorganized one, but they do make it a problem to describe, understand, and lead.

How bad is it? Consider the following excerpt from a May 1995 article in *Fortune* magazine by Shawn Tully:

> Here's a line of business whose customer base is shrinking. Rivals battle for market share by offering deep discounts. If they hold the line on prices, they risk losing out to cheaper, state-subsidized competitors. Their physical plants are falling apart. They can't fire their highest-paid workers—who put in far less than 40-hour workweeks—and federal law says that even the laggards never have to retire.
>
> Sound pretty bad? It gets worse. The CEO isn't free to run the business; he or she needs the workers' approval for most major decisions. The pressures of managing-by-compromise force most bosses to depart within four years. As Thomas Hobbes, the 17th-century English philosopher, put it, their lives are nasty, brutish, and short.
>
> Welcome to the Byzantine business of higher education.

While some may argue that the article in *Fortune* overgeneralizes—and it probably does—there are myriad other individuals, organizations, and associations with a similar take on the challenges, especially those involving leadership, that face higher education.

The April 1996 *Policy Perspectives* from the Pew Higher Education Roundtable focused almost exclusively on decision-making and responsibility in higher education. The Roundtable notes that "however justified the academy may consider itself to be in slowing its own transformation, the political and economic as well as cultural pressures for change have now grown more punitive. Voices from all quarters are calling for a reexamination of what institutions do and how they do it in light of the realities of the 20th century. In the minds of critics, as well as many supporters, there is no reason why higher education should hold itself aloof from the need to serve customers, to supply wants rather than define needs, or to pursue and husband the resources with the same assiduousness as other businesses."

When I think about how some, perhaps many, faculty and administrators react to decision-making, I am reminded of the words of Charles Handy. Writing in *The Age of Paradox*, Handy notes that "people clamor for rights but ignore their responsibilities, want democracy but expect others to sort out all its problems for them, complain when others take initiative but take no initiative themselves."

According to the Pew *Policy Perspectives*, "it is the campus executive . . . who is caught between societal pressure for change and the faculty's wish to maintain the academy in the form they have known. Administrators are charged by their faculty to afford protection from the very pressures that the institution's external constituencies are, with increasing resolve, bringing to bear."

Some may say this is an unduly pessimistic appraisal of campus decision-making. But those of us who have worked at colleges and universities recognize the reality of these words.

The need for leadership

There is only one legitimate response to the problems facing higher education: strong leadership. Leadership committed to listening widely and carefully, to thinking critically, to planning strategically, and to acting boldly.

Burt Nanus, in *The Leader's Edge: The Seven Keys to Leadership in a Turbulent World*, notes that leaders take charge, make things happen, dream dreams, and then translate those dreams into reality. Nanus goes on to say that "leaders attract the voluntary commitment of followers, energize them, and transform organizations into new entities with greater potential for survival, growth, and excellence. Effective leadership empowers an organization to maximize its contribution to the well-being of its members and the larger society of which it is a part. If managers are known for their skills in solving problems, then leaders are known for being masters in designing and building institutions—they are the architects of the organization's future."

The problem with paradigms

It is very difficult to discuss leadership at any level—even such a cursory examination as laid out here—without discussing paradigms.

A paradigm is an accepted way of looking at something on the basis of experience, background, and perception. As you may know from experience, paradigms are both stabilizing and debilitating. A paradigm can provide stability, but it can also shield you too long from necessary change and adaptation.

Table 2-1.
Old Paradigms in Higher Education

The demographic downturn is nearly over, and soon the pool of traditional-age students will increase in size.

The majority of students anticipate attending college full-time.

Private higher education will continue to be perceived as of generally higher quality than public higher education.

Public institutions will soon receive substantial increases in state dollars.

Alumni will continue to support the institutions from which they received their first degree.

Student success is determined by grades.

Campus life will center around athletics and clubs.

Most students are interested in a traditional liberal arts, residential, classroom-based education.

Corporations and foundations will continue to support higher education at a substantial level.

The marketplace will continue to absorb double-digit tuition increases.

Joel Barker, writing in *Future Edge*, points out that new paradigms put everyone practicing the old paradigm at great risk. The higher one's position, the greater the risk. The better you are at your paradigm, the more you have invested in it, the more you have to lose by changing paradigms. Barker reminds us that when we are in the middle of a paradigm, it is hard to imagine any other. As one cartoonist noted simply, "Shift happens."

One of the great ironies in higher education is that most administrators and faculty who make decisions remember, as their pivotal paradigm, their own college experience—an experience that holds true for fewer and fewer students each year. They remember dorms, not residence halls. They remember going to school full-time. They remember campus life vibrant with activities and athletics. They remember a college experience that many of today's—and tomorrow's—students will simply never experience for themselves.

Many administrators and faculty believe the paradigms listed in Table 2-1 still define higher education even though data and recent experiences suggest that a shift has occurred.

Leadership roles

According to Karl Albrecht in *The Northbound Train: Finding the Purpose, Setting the Direction, Shaping the Destiny of Your Organization*, today's leaders have four distinct roles:

1. **The leader as visionary:** creates meaning by crafting the vision, mission, and direction that define the focus of the enterprise.
2. **The leader as team-builder:** puts the right people in the right places for the top-level leadership team, welds them into a single-minded core of advocacy for the common cause, capitalizes on their individual strengths and resources, and continually develops them as team and individual leaders who can serve the mandate required of them.
3. **The leader as a living symbol:** the individual who "walks the talk" in a highly visible way, demonstrating not necessarily a charismatic style of leadership but a constant and unrelenting pattern of reinforcing the institution's vision.
4. **The leader as buck-stopper:** faces the difficult issues, discerns the truth of challenges, and makes the tough decisions and dramatic changes that have to be made. While this involves open-minded listening and collaboration with the leadership team, it is the leader who must ultimately face the music and manage the organization's response to critical issues.

Visionaries as leaders

Burt Nanus, writing in *Visionary Leadership*, views leaders in a slightly different way. While he agrees that there are four dimensions, his are oriented toward inside and outside environment and present and future domains. Figure 2-1 outlines these domains.

The *Direction-setter* selects and articulates the target in the future external environment toward which the organization should direct its energies. This is the meaning of vision. To be a good direction-setter, you must be able to set a course toward a destination that others will recognize as representing real progress for the organization.

The *Change Agent* is responsible for catalyzing changes in the internal environment. To be a good change agent, you must be able to articulate developments in the outside world, assess their implications for your institution, create the sense of urgency and priority for changes that your vision requires in light of these developments, promote experimentation, and empower people to make the necessary changes. You must also be able to build flexibility into your organization and operations and encourage prudent risk-taking.

The *Spokesperson*—as a skilled speaker, a concerned listener, and the very embodiment of the organization's vision—is the chief advocate and negotiator for the organization and its vision with outside constituencies. To be an effective spokesperson, you must be the major negotiator with other organizations and the builder of networks of external relationships to provide useful ideas, resources, support, or information for your organization. You—and your vision—must become both the medium and the message that express what is worthwhile, attractive, and exciting about the future of your organization.

The *Coach* is a team-builder who empowers individuals in the organization and passionately "lives the vision," thereby serving as a mentor and example for those whose efforts are necessary to make the vision become reality.

These four roles—direction-setter, change agent, spokesperson, and coach—together define the job of the visionary leader. They are all equally important, and no one can be a successful leader without excelling at all of them.

Figure 2-1.
Leadership Domains

External Environment

Spokesperson	*Direction-setter*
Present	Future
Coach	*Change Agent*

Internal Environment

Leaders as planners

Traditionally, most leaders have seen their job as developing logical, beautiful, nicely presented schemes and scenarios. Working in front of a word processor or spreadsheet, they tend, as George Keller notes in *Academic Strategy*, to overlook or at least underappreciate people's egos, politics, tradition, and the need to have their plans enacted. Leaders as planners were often much more concerned with getting the plan written than achieving the plan's goals.

But not anymore. The new wave of leaders, the leaders who have as their overarching goal the success of the institution, are more interested in getting good things done than with merely conceiving them. They are interested in results—function rather than simply form.

Where plans begin – a renewed sense of mission

All marketing plans and strategies must be founded on the institution's mission—its *raison d'être*. Marketing plans must be a logical and even heartfelt extension of an institution's mission. If the mission and planning efforts are not in congruence, then something is deeply flawed. It is destructive to the institution and deceptive to the marketplace to develop and execute a plan that is inconsistent with the institution's mission. Not surprisingly, such efforts at reconciling fundamental incongruencies will, and should, fail.

Missions describe founding principles and philosophies, people and events. Missions describe what was important once and still is. Missions describe core, shared values—values the campus community has decided are unassailable. As such, when an incongruency between an institution's mission and its marketing plan arises, the mission is seldom at fault. More often than not, campus administrators, perhaps responding to a crisis, have launched a quick fix. Without taking the time to look inward at their mission, they have chosen to act. And when a new crisis occurs or another opportunity arises, they will act again, caring little that their actions and reactions, without the stabilizing influence of the institution's mission, are whipping the institution first in one direction and then in another.

Figure 2-2.
Marketing, Mission, Vision, and Strategy

Vision as direction

Your mission is an essential declaration of purpose. But that's not enough: You also need vision—a sense of where you want to go. John Bryson, in *Strategic Planning for Public and Nonprofit Organizations*, notes that missions must be expanded in a "vision of success." Whereas your mission clarifies an organization's purpose, or why it should be doing what it does, vision clarifies what the organization should look like as it fulfills its mission. Mission statements are descriptive; vision statements are prophetic. Missions are instructive; visions are inspiring. Mission statements are printed in the catalog or hung on a wall. Vision statements are told and lived in the soul of the institution and its followers.*

As Figure 2-2 suggests, vision is founded on an institution's mission. In today's complex environment, vision is more important than ever. The myriad options and opportunities before today's colleges and universities often distract and entice, confound and confuse. Vision provides a sense of direction in this sometimes difficult landscape.

The need for vision

Nanus, as noted earlier, defines vision as "a realistic, credible, attractive future for your organization." He goes on to say that there is no more powerful engine driving an organization toward excellence and long-range success than an attractive, worthwhile, and achievable vision of the future that is widely shared.

Karl Albrecht uses a metaphor, "the northbound train," to describe how impor-

---

*Many of these insights and thoughts on vision were outlined in an unpublished paper by Dr. Robert Smith, Dean of Arts and Sciences at the University of Tennessee, Martin. This paper is quoted at length and with permission on the following pages.

tant vision is to an organization. Albrecht says that this image from his book *The Northbound Train* conveys an unwavering commitment to a particular direction. "Think about the implications of a northbound train: purpose and direction," he says.

> No vision statement or mission statement can ever make much sense unless it originates in some valid concept about what it takes to succeed. It is not a platitude. It is not a slogan. It is not an exercise in journalism; it is an exercise in careful, clear, creative, disciplined, and mature thought. It provides a critical success premise that leaders can understand, commit to, and dramatize to others. The idea of a moving train also conveys a strong sense of momentum, of unstoppable, implacable movement in an unambiguous direction.

Albrecht notes that leaders and followers must have a clear image of this northbound train. The key word is image—something that you can describe and that people can see in their mind's eye. It is a mental picture of an enterprise, operating in an environment, performing to some criterion of excellence, and appreciated for what it contributes. He writes:

> Vision statements are living elements of the institution full of their own challenges. They are kept alive by repetition in everyday activities and by rewarding efforts consistent with the vision. Therefore, leaders have to tie the vision to the work of the followers so the followers can see what role they have in achieving the vision and how important they are to achieving the vision.

Vision as catalyst

How important is a shared vision of success to a college or university? Borrowing from Bryson, Nanus, and others, we can quickly determine the powerful and essential benefits of a strong vision:

- The right vision attracts commitment and energizes people.
- The right vision creates meaning in people's lives.
- The right vision establishes a standard of excellence.
- Organization members are given specific, reasonable, and supportive guidance about what is expected of them and why. Stakeholders see how they fit into the big picture.
- A vision helps clarify the organization's definition of success and desirable behavior, thereby helping people discriminate among preferred and undesirable actions and outcomes.
- An articulated vision lessens internal debate and helps the institution focus its resources and energy. Less time will be expended on debating what to do, how to do it, and why, and more time can be devoted simply to getting on with the institution's business. An agreed-upon vision may contribute to a significant reduction in organizational conflict.
- A clear vision of success provides an effective substitute for leadership. When the vision is clear, there is less need for someone to point the way continually; people are more able and inclined to lead and manage themselves.

■ A vision can be inspirational and motivating. If a vision of success becomes a calling, an enormous amount of individual energy and dedication can be released in pursuit of a forceful vision.

Nanus introduces the reader to Charles Garfield, a computer scientist who has written extensively about what he calls "mission psychology." Garfield worked at NASA in the Apollo 11 era and well remembers the intense fervor with which people worked toward the one superordinate goal they all understood. President John F. Kennedy declared it in 1961 when he stated, "I believe that this nation should commit itself to achieving the goal, before this decade is out, of landing a man on the moon and returning him safely to Earth."

Kennedy's declaration became the manifesto, the organizing principle that gave meaning and direction not only to the space program but to the professional lives of many creative technical people in government and the aerospace industry. Says Garfield, "I had never seen such a group of people work with such absolute focus and fervor as those people, who saw it as their own personal mission to send astronauts to the moon. They worked incredibly long hours, under intense pressure, and they loved it."

Colleges and universities would benefit greatly from a vision that captivates their campus communities as much as the vision to place a man on the moon captivated our nation.

Vision in higher education

Are there visions in higher education that can foster a mission psychology? Are there visions that captivate, inspire, and galvanize? Consider the following three:

■ We will be a premier Catholic liberal arts institution, educating thinkers with principles. — Small, urban Catholic college
■ We will establish Houston Baptist University as America's premier, urban Christian university in next seven to ten years.
■ We will be clearly established and recognized as a comprehensive public university which, through teaching, research, and public service, becomes a center for higher education in the nation. — Urban regional four-year institution

Determining whether you need a (new) vision

Although there is no simple way to ascertain whether your vision is still doing the job, there are some warning signs that your current one may no longer be adequate. First, according to Nanus, is evidence of confusion about purpose. Do your key people frequently disagree about your direction, your target audiences, or your overall purpose? Second is pessimism about the future or cynicism about the present. Do faculty, staff, and administrators complain about few challenges or a lack of fun?

Is the college or university losing legitimacy, market share and position, or its reputation for innovation? Are other campuses doing a better job meeting the needs of students you once served?

Does your college or university seem out of touch with trends in the environment? Do trustees or advisory groups suggest you might have lost a bit of your edge or might not be keeping up with changes in the marketplace, in education, and in teaching technology?

Are there signs of a decline in pride? Are committee assignments slipping, routine meetings skipped, deadlines missed?

Is there excessive risk-avoidance, with people abiding in, and sometimes taking shelter behind, narrow job descriptions, unwilling to accept responsibility for new projects or resisting change?

Is there no shared sense of progress or momentum? Is it difficult for some of your department heads to articulate how much things are improving? Do they still feel they have an attractive future with the institution?

Is there a hyperactive rumor mill, with people constantly trying to find out through the grapevine what is in store for them or the organization? Is the grapevine more likely to be believed than formal communication from senior administrators?

The vision process

Though the president is often the catalyst for vision, an institution's vision is seldom created by a single person. Generally, there are two approaches to developing a vision. The first approach is relatively autocratic, the second more consensual. The challenge, of course, is deciding which approach is best for you and your institution.

If your institution is in peril and significant internal and external stakeholders recognize the need for timely action, then it is more permissible for a president—after a careful analysis of the institution, its audiences (both internal and external), and the marketplace—to declare a vision.

However, if the institution has a history of consensual decision-making, and if faculty, staff, administrators, and even students are often involved in debating issues and setting priorities, then an autocratic vision process will not work. Internal and external stakeholders must be involved.

There is an important rule about establishing a vision that must not be overlooked. In the absence of a recognized crisis, if you fail to involve internal and external stakeholders in creating the vision, you run the risk of that vision's never taking hold. Remember, a campus culture will almost always outlast its leadership.

Says Robert Smith:

> An institution in crisis, moving in the wrong direction, or without a reserve of talented potential leaders will not likely develop a shared vision without the forceful persuasive powers of the single leader. In this culture, the leader may have to set the tone, direction, and specifics of a vision for others to follow.
>
> However, some cultures have a core set of values, direction, and a sense of purpose but lack unified focus and commitment to action. In this culture, the leader resurrects a vision from the other team members and, using shared ownership, brings focus and direction to

the organization. This approach recognizes that frustration, alienation, disillusion, and morale are closely tied to a lack of shared vision.

Once the college or university has a team-derived and focused vision statement, then the energy is focused on achieving the vision.

Properties of a good vision

Sometimes a vision just feels right. Other visions are less obvious. Generally, however, the right vision for a college or university should be

- Future-oriented,
- Utopian—clearly offering a better future for the organization,
- Appropriate—consistent with mission, history, values, and culture,
- Reflecting high ideals and standards of excellence,
- Clear in purpose and direction,
- Able to inspire enthusiasm and encourage commitment, and
- Ambitious.

Negotiating the vision

> "The issue is not usually a lack of visions but the institution's will and resolve to declare a single vision and stick with it."

After working with a number of colleges and universities, I believe that vision often becomes an extension, even a personification, of the president. On the other hand, as Jeffrey Pfeffer noted in several of his books (see bibliography, page 207), visions are often coalitional—something to be negotiated among rival coalitions. A committee of six well-intended faculty, administrators, and alumni can easily come up with half a dozen distinctive visions. The issue is not usually a lack of visions but the institution's will and resolve to declare a single vision and stick with it. Bryson, based on an interview with Lonnie Hegelson, reminds us that to construct a compelling vision, decision-makers must be courageous. They must envision and listen to their best selves. And they must be disciplined enough to affirm the vision in the present and to work hard to make it real in the here and now.

This is a ticklish issue. Even in an age of egalitarianism drawn from a tradition of collegiality, one individual—the president—is ultimately responsible for institutional vision. It is her or his responsibility to assess internal coalitions and external opportunities and obstacles and then declare a direction. It is her or his responsibility to provide the impetus to vision.

Regardless of the process, or how much the vision is shared, some factions will always object. Some will detract. Some may even seek to undermine. Keller, writing in *Academic Strategy*, reminds us that although consensus will never be achieved, neither should active dissent be allowed: "Participation is imperative. There need not be full consensus; there seldom is. Dissent must be permitted, although sabotage should not be."

Articulating the vision to the campus community

A vision must be articulated to the entire campus community before it acquires the force necessary to change an organization and move it in an intended direction.

Vision not shared is not vision.

The key to gaining widespread commitment to a new vision is to present it in such a way that people want to participate and will freely choose to do so. This does not begin with the simple communication of a declared vision but must be a salient element of the overall visioning process.

I well remember making a presentation before a president and his five chief administrators. I asked whether the institution had a vision for success. All nodded. I then asked them each to take out a piece of paper and write out the vision. As I read them aloud, it was clear that the vision was not as shared or communicated as they thought. I also remember visiting Baylor University a few years ago. I asked a member of the grounds crew if he knew Baylor's vision. "Sure," he said, "I have a copy of it right here." The man pulled a laminated card from his shirt pocket. On it was Baylor's mission and vision.

Modeling the way

In *The Leadership Challenge*, James M. Kouzes and Barry Poser write that at a faculty convocation at Santa Clara University, the president, Reverend William J. Rewak, S.J., spoke eloquently about the changes anticipated for the campus. After he showed slides of planned new buildings and gardens, he said: "Vision needs management, electricity, and concrete." Grand dreams, he reminded us, cannot become significant realities with *élan* alone. Leaders also must have detailed plans. They must steer projects along the course, measure performance, raise funds, and take corrective action. Many conventional management practices are certainly useful. Yet there is an even more demanding leadership task if a person is to direct the course of action. The leader must model the way.

> **"Leaders get others to buy into their dreams..."**

Quick Glance

Readings on Mission, Vision, and Leadership

To help gain a greater sense of the enabling power of mission, vision, leadership, and organizational change, consider reading the following:

- Albrecht, Karl: *The Northbound Train: Finding the Purpose, Setting the Direction, Shaping the Destiny of Your Organizations*
- Bryson, John: *Strategic Planning for Public and Nonprofit Organizations*
- Clemens, John K., and Mayer, Douglas F.: *The Classic Touch: Lessons in Leadership from Homer to Hemingway*
- Dalziel, Murray M., and Schoonover, Stephen C.: *Changing Ways: A Practical Tool for Implementing Change Within Organizations*
- Kouzes, James M., and Posner, Barry: *The Leadership Challenge: How to Get Extraordinary Things Done in Organizations* and *Credibility: How Leaders Gain and Lose It, Why People Demand It*
- Keller, George: *Academic Strategy*
- Naisbitt, John: *Reinventing the Corporation*
- Peters, Tom: *In Search of Excellence: Lessons from America's Best-Run Companies*
- Safire, William, and Safir, Leonard: *Leadership*

Kouzes and Posner go on to say that leaders *inspire a shared vision.* They breathe life into others' hopes and dreams and enable them to see the exciting possibilities the future holds. Leaders get others to buy into their dreams by showing how all will be served by a common purpose.

In some ways, leaders live their lives backwards. They envision results even before they have started their projects, much as an architect draws a blueprint or an engineer builds a model. Their clear image of the future pulls them forward. But visions seen only by leaders are insufficient to create significant change or an organized movement. A person with no followers is not a leader, and people will not become followers until they accept a vision as their own. You cannot command commitment; you can only inspire it.

A vision with heart

According to Kouzes and Posner, there is one other aspect of leadership and vision—the encouragement that leaders give themselves. One leader, when asked why he worked so hard, said, "I love to turn the key in the door and put on the coffeepot." Not only must leaders encourage the hearts of their followers; they must take time and care to encourage their own hearts as well.

3

A New Perspective on Marketing

"I keep marketing for the same reason that the pilot of an airplane keeps his engines running once he is off the ground."

—William Wrigley, Jr., when asked why he kept marketing his chewing gum even though it was already the most popular in the world

An expanded definition of marketing

A successful marketing effort often begins with a redefinition of marketing. All too often, colleges and universities focus almost exclusively on the promotional aspect of marketing, and it is this limited definition that is usually at the root of both their distrust of the process and their underestimation of its potential benefits. In the minds of administrators, staff, and faculty, a promotion-only definition of marketing leads only to gimmickry and hyperbole. Marketing at this level is often distilled to the notion of buying a bigger billboard or creating slick publications.

A proper definition of marketing is more dynamic, contemplative, balanced, and inclusive. Philip Kotler defines marketing as:

> The analysis, planning, implementation, and control of carefully formulated programs designed to bring about voluntary exchanges of values with target markets for the purpose of achieving organizational objectives.

Although this definition may at first appear cumbersome, it is actually quite elegant. Let's take a few minutes to dissect this definition.

Analysis and planning. Successful marketing efforts are based on a careful, research-based appraisal of an institution's internal and external environment. Not whim, not rose-colored glasses, but careful, thoughtful, and ongoing research.

Implementation and control of carefully formulated programs. The carefully formulated programs are the four Ps: product, price, place, and promotion. The four Ps are the heart of marketing. While most administrators are comfortable with the notion of marketing as promotion, they often overlook the role product, price, and place can play in an institution's marketing effort.

Voluntary exchange of values. The primary goal of marketing is to help the institution establish exchange relationships with key publics. Donors and students and alumni must be willing to exchange their values (dollars and time) for values offered by the institution (quality, reputation, prestige, outcomes, earning potential, etc.). Ideally, as an institution's marketing efforts succeed, target audiences will actually seek out this exchange relationship, and the institution will spend less time and money persuading people to trade values. Stanford University, for instance, spends less time than it used to at recruiting students; many more students seek out Stanford than can possibly attend. Students interested in attending actively seek to exchange their values—dollars, time, and commitment—with the values of a Stanford education—quality and opportunity.

Target audiences. Marketing efforts are most often directed at changing the behavior of people—in this case students, community residents, donors, or any group of individuals on whom the institution depends or with whom it must interact.

Achieve organizational objectives. Though colleges and universities have diverse organizational objectives, all institutions depend on resources, primarily dollars, to sustain quality and diversity. Every institution must direct sufficient marketing efforts to facilitating the flow of tuition, tax, and donated dollars into the institution.

The four Ps

As stated earlier, the four Ps represent the four variables that institutions manipulate as part of their marketing and positioning strategy. Sometimes the four Ps are called the marketing mix. This definition is helpful because it reminds us that the four Ps are the ingredients we mix to develop specific messages for specific target audiences.

Product

The first P is product. Not surprisingly, there is great confusion about what an institution's product is. Some believe a college or university's product is what is taught in the classroom. Others believe it is students. Still others think a product is what a student does with her or his degree. Although all of these definitions capture a dimension of product, especially from a recruiting perspective, they also limit the impact that product has in marketing. For our purposes, we will define a college or university's product as:

> **The sum of an institution's academic, social, physical, and values/spiritual**

dimensions and the opportunities that are available to graduates.

This can get complicated in a hurry, so we should spend a little time here. Ultimately, there are two ways in which to view product mix: first, how the institution decides to mix different aspects of its academic, social, physical, and values/spiritual dimensions, and second, how external target audiences perceive and value this mix.

Mixing the product

One of the most wonderful aspects of American higher education is the tremendous

---

Quick Glance

From the FOUR Ps to the FOUR Cs and Beyond

Any discussion of the four Ps is extraordinarily useful, especially as colleges and universities seek to expand their understanding of marketing from promotion to the other three Ps: product, price, and place. However, it is important to note that even as an understanding of the four Ps evolves, so do the four Ps themselves.

Historically, the four Ps are written from a top-down perspective. In other words, the organization, in this case a college or university, "knows" what's best for students (product), charges what it wishes or needs to (price), and offers its product largely where it wishes (place). In fact, the only real customization, and it is limited, occurs with promotion. We occasionally segment or customize messages or appeals to different kinds of students or donors.

Nearly 10 years ago, the traditional downward approach of the four Ps was challenged with the creation of the four Cs by Don Schultz and Bob Lauterborn. Instead of product, Schultz and Lauterborn offer us consumer. Instead of price, we have cost. Instead of place, we have convenience. And instead of promotion, we have communication.

Where the four Ps have a top-down orientation, the four Cs focus on the needs of the customer or, in this case, on the consumer. An understanding of the four Cs is extremely helpful because this orientation stresses a dynamic marketplace and a strong interest in meeting customer needs. With a four-Cs approach, there is more likely to be real segmentation of product, price, place, and, of course, promotion.

But things keep changing. We have seen a flurry of other books on marketing that address the influence of the customer. Don Schultz, Stanley Tannenbaum, and Robert Lauterborn's *Integrated Marketing Communications: The New Marketing Paradigm* in 1993 emphasized integrated marketing communication—the need to customize message strategies for each customer or at least each major segment. There is Terry Vavra's *Aftermarketing*, which stresses long-term relationships to customers (not simply potential customers). Regis McKenna's *Relationship Marketing*, and Edward Nash's *Database Marketing: The Ultimate Marketing Tool*, and Edward Burnett's *Database Marketing: The New Profit Frontier* take varied approaches to the same goal: knowing the customer.

It is not surprising, then, that Don Peppers and Martha Rogers have taken things to their logical extreme. With their publication of *Enterprise One to One: Tools for Competing in the Interactive Age*, they make the case that successful organizations must customize their products to reflect the needs of each customer and that an understanding of their needs is based not on predicted data but on data that describe actual behavior.

Integrated marketing communication, relationship marketing, and one-to-one marketing have two significant attributes. First, they all stress aggressive listening. And second, they stress not just a willingness but a desire to customize.

Are colleges and universities ever likely to develop one-to-one relationships? It's doubtful. But even if they fall short, any movement toward a customer orientation built on aggressive listening and product customization will likely pay tremendous benefits.

---

diversity of product mix. For example, MIT has a different product mix than Yakima Valley Community College, and Eastern Oklahoma State College certainly has a different product mix than Bethel College in Minnesota or Widener University in Philadelphia. Students and donors both understand that these five institutions are quite dissimilar. They are dissimilar, in part, by how they have chosen to emphasize different aspects of their product.

How an institution chooses to mix its product should depend on its founding mission and how the president interprets that mission and articulates it through her or his vision. However, the product mix should also recognize and even anticipate market realities. An institution may have a product mix that has served it well for 100 years. But changes in the numbers, composition, or interests of students or donors may require that it reexamine the mix.

Colleges and universities are often in a dilemma at this point. Some institutions, responding to each trend in the marketplace, appear to change their product mix at the drop of a hat. Others ignore significant changes in their marketplace and persist with a product mix that is antiquated and unappealing. Smart colleges and universities must find a balance between these two extremes.

How target audiences perceive and value the mix

Different audiences often expect a product with different emphases: Students are often interested in different aspects of an institution than their parents are, and alumni donors are often interested in different aspects than major donors are. Table 3-1 is an oversimplification of how one college might mix aspects of its product.

Of course, the key to creating an effective product mix is to conduct research to determine audiences' expectations, then mix the product within the range of possibilities established by your mission and vision.

A missed opportunity

One of the most important dimensions of your product mix, especially for student recruiting, is your curriculum. Many colleges and universities fail to use their curriculum to differentiate themselves from the competition. From the perspective of students and donors alike, too many offer the same programs in the same ways. Business and industry use a matrix—called the product life cycle—to describe the logical outcome of too many businesses trying to sell the same product in the same marketplace. The product life cycle describes an important yet often overlooked phenomenon: As more and more companies offer the same product to the same market, the amount of money that businesses can charge customers for that product will drop.

Colleges and universities are facing what might be termed a curriculum life cycle—too many schools offering the exact same courses and programs as their competition and teaching these courses and programs in the exact same way.

As you can see from Table 3-2, as more campuses offer the same programs and courses, students will begin to make decisions on the basis of cost. This is particularly

Table 3-1.

Possible Product-mix Emphases at One Institution

Target Audience	Product-mix Emphases
Prospective students	Strong emphasis on academics and social life
Parents	Strong emphasis on academics, less emphasis on social life
Alumni donors	Less emphasis on academics and stronger emphasis on social life and athletics
Major donors	Stronger emphasis on academics

true of undergraduate students and somewhat less true of graduate students.

If you examine your curriculum, you are likely to find that most of your programs and courses are at either market maturity or sales decline. Very few colleges and universities offer a meaningful number of Stage One or Stage Two programs or courses.

Consider the following example. In the mid- to late 1970s, a very small number of institutions began offering computer science programs. These Stage One programs attracted a great deal of attention. Both students and donors were interested. Through the 1980s, as more and more institutions began offering computer science, the market continued to grow and then mature. Finally, the market has begun to decline.

It is very important to consider carefully how you can use your curriculum to differentiate yourself from your competition in meaningful ways. You must offer courses and programs that no one else in your marketplace is offering. Or you must offer similar courses and programs in ways that students and donors will find attractive. As your curriculum matures, you must always be scanning the marketplace to anticipate new curriculum trends—not fads, but meaningful responses to how your marketplace is changing.

Questions you should ask related to product:

- What is our product?
- How can we more effectively mix our academic, social, physical, and spiritual products?
- What aspects of our product most interest donors, alumni, and community residents?
- How does our product compare with those at competing institutions?
- Is/are our product/programs in demand? How do we know?
- Will students and donors overcome real and imagined barriers to take advantage of our product?
- What are the demonstrated outcomes of our product?

Price

The second P is price. Traditionally, colleges and universities have focused on only one aspect of price: the cost in dollars to attend and a derivative of cost, financial aid. However, price plays a much larger role in marketing than most realize because a true definition of price includes both dollars and nondollar costs.

Let's examine these important concepts for a moment.

Student recruiting and price

First, let's look at student recruiting. Students are very interested in the bottom-line cost in dollars. However, students must also struggle with sometimes significant nondollar costs. For example, suppose the institution is in an unattractive area; students will perceive this as a cost. Or perhaps, from students' perspective, it is too large, too small, too Catholic, or not Catholic enough. These and dozens of other variables may also be calculated as costs—nondollar costs, but costs nonetheless.

Table 3-2
Curriculum Life Cycle

Stage 1
Market Introduction
Pioneer program with no competition—price is not an issue

Stage 2
Market Growth
One or more colleges in a market offer the same program—price is becoming an issue

Stage 3
Market Maturity
Many competing colleges in a market offer the same program—students are more likely to differentiate programs by price

Stage 4
Sales Decline
Students cannot differentiate programs and choose the less expensive

There is a curious relationship between nondollar costs and product mix. If a student is not satisfied with some aspect of your product, that dissatisfaction is translated into a nondollar cost. For example, while the quality of the faculty is a primary component of academic product, if students feel that faculty are unavailable to them as first-year students, students will translate that product into a nondollar cost.

Interestingly, the cumulative impact of these nondollar costs often has a greater impact on the final decision of where to attend college than do dollar costs. Dollar costs may help establish the cohort of potential colleges, but calculation of nondollar costs often helps students decide which they will attend.

It's crucial to address nondollar costs in a systematic way. Though most institutions can do little to change the cost to attend without sinking significant dollars into financial aid, they can often do much to manage nondollar costs. Consider the graph in Figure 3-1, which represents data from a survey of prospective students. The graph, using a gap-analysis format, actually depicts paired data sets for each variable. The bar on the left for each data set indicates, on a scale of one to nine, how much students value a certain characteristic or variable. The paired bar on the right is students' evaluation of how well they feel the college does on that variable. Look, for example, at the paired bars for advising. Students rate the importance of advising very highly (about 8.2 out of nine). However, they feel that the college, overall, does not offer a great advising program (rating it only 4.1 out of nine). The size of this gap indicates an opportunity for the college to address a nondollar cost.

Fund raising and price

Donors often have a different perspective on price than do students and parents. From the donor's perspective, price issues are more often nondollar than dollar. Donors, for example, want to know that the college is well-managed, that it is true to its founding mission, and that the president has an articulated vision. In other words,

Figure 3-1.
Students' Ratings of College Characteristics

Source: Stamats Communications, Inc.

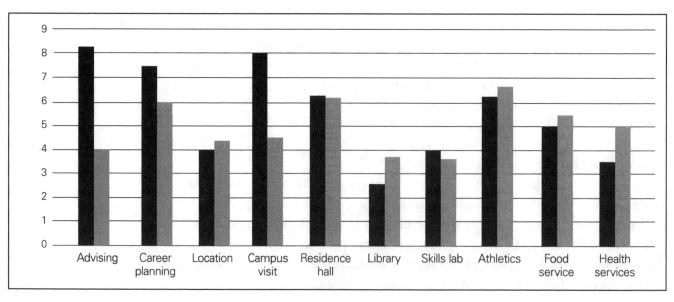

donors want to ally themselves with institutions that are moving ahead.

Questions you should ask related to price:

- How much do we charge for our product?
- How does this cost compare with competing institutions'?
- How effective is our financial aid program?
- What nondollar costs are associated with our product?
- What strategies have we implemented to determine, evaluate, and negate nondollar costs?
- What nondollar costs most concern alumni and donors?

Balance the scale

Before we continue our discussion of the remaining four Ps, we need to examine a subtle but important aspect of price—value. Whenever we consider the cost of something, we also calculate, perhaps subconsciously, what we will get in return. We want to make sure we are getting a good deal for our money or time. We call this good deal "value"—the relationship between the cost of something and the benefits we will receive.

It is very important that we completely understand the relationship between costs and benefits. Let's look at how this relationship affects how we make decisions. People, including students, add up the perceived dollar and nondollar costs of doing something, then add up the perceived benefits. If the costs outweigh the benefits, we don't do it, because we are not getting a good deal. But if the benefits outweigh the costs, we do it, because we are getting a good deal. When students say, "You cost too much," what they are really saying is that you are not worth the cost—the value isn't there—they do not perceive enough benefits for the costs they must incur.

Donors also understand the relationship between costs and benefits. When they decide not to donate, it is seldom over a dollar-cost concern. More likely they are concerned about nondollar issues: about being identified with a particular campaign or institution, about a drain on their time, or about being inconvenienced. However, if the benefit of donating is significantly large, the cost/benefit scale will swing in favor of a donation; prospective donors will find value in their relationship with the institution.

Smart institutions understand the relationship between costs and benefits. Research is conducted with each major target audience to discover how it perceives the costs and benefits of its relationship with the institution. Benefits are created and promoted, while costs are addressed and, if possible, negated. The sense of value is heightened to facilitate the exchange relationship.

Place

Of the four Ps, place is often the most underused. Historically, place has been bound to geography—the physical spot where a college or university does what it does. Of late, however, place has been expanded to include time, or when a college or university does what it does.

Quick Glance

Financial aid Information
While most institutions cannot significantly increase the amount of aid or discount tuition, they can often improve the quality and timeliness of the information about financial aid, and they can certainly improve the level of service in the financial aid office. This will often have as much or more effect on financial aid than just increasing the amount of money that is available.

Place has also been affected greatly by multimedia, distance learning, cable TV, and other electronic wonders that allow institutions to shift place and time. "Over the next few years, as more and more colleges and universities develop viable links to the emerging information highway, place may become a moot point," says Robert Smith at the University of Tennessee, Martin. "The handful of institutions that currently offer courses and degrees via electronic media will explode rapidly, and the day will quickly arise that any student anywhere may tap into the information highway and obtain a degree from virtually any college or university in the country."

Target audiences will position place as one of the following:

■ A positive attribute of the institution
■ A negative attribute
■ A neutral attribute

If your target audiences perceive your place as prestigious, rich in resources, or fun, this positive view can be a powerful part of your marketing mix. You can use place to offset other parts of your marketing mix that target audiences find less attractive. For example, suppose your facilities are not terrific. You might help balance this weakness by emphasizing your great location.

However, if your place is rightly viewed as inconvenient, distant, or unsafe, the overall impact of place is negative and you need to emphasize the other Ps instead: price, product, and promotion.

Finally, if target audiences are ambivalent about place, you must emphasize those aspects of place that are beneficial while balancing the less beneficial aspects by emphasizing other attributes of your institution.

The best way to evaluate your place is to ask target audiences the effect place played in decisions they made. You may discover, for instance, that rather than assembling on your main campus, students are more willing to attend classes at other sites. Donors, rather than traveling to an out-of-the-way college in west Texas, will gladly attend receptions you sponsor in Dallas or Fort Worth.

It is possible to change how your target audiences view your place. I remember a publication from a consortium of colleges and universities in northern Ohio that sought to position their place, Cleveland, as a great benefit. "Some colleges have pretty ponds," the copy exclaimed, "while we have a great lake." The piece then went on to discuss the many resources available in Cleveland including world-class internships, entertainment, and cultural opportunities.

Questions you should ask related to place:

■ Where are our programs and events offered?
■ Are people willing to take classes and attend events in those places?
■ Do people find these places inviting, attractive, convenient, and safe?
■ What segments of our target market perceive our location as positive; what segments perceive it as negative?
■ What other places might serve us better?
■ What alternative, electronic-based delivery modes are available?

■ Are our programs offered at a time that students, donors, and other target audiences find attractive?

■ Does this place or time compete with other potential conflicts (job, family obligations, traffic patterns)?

Promotion

The final P is promotion. In many respects, promotion involves marketing the other three Ps through such avenues as advertising, publications, direct mail, personal contact, and environmentals. In other words, promotion involves bringing a mix of your product, price, and place attributes to the attention of your target audiences.

It is this final P, promotion, that usually causes colleges and universities the most grief. Many faculty, staff, and administrators believe that being good at something is all it takes to flourish in today's marketplace. These people often believe that marketing and promotion are unethical on one hand and superficial on the other.

A promotion-only definition of marketing is the cause of this problem. A true marketing effort involves creating a product that is valued, at a price that people will pay, in a place to which people will come. But the fourth ingredient, promotion, is the catalyst. Your product, price, and place must be brought to people's attention through promotion.

Colleges and universities that seek to develop a strong promotion plan have a breathtaking array of options at their disposal. Even a small list would include such strategies as those in Table 3-3.

To help focus your media strategies, it is useful to ask target audiences which general and specific media they are most likely to respond to. For example, alumni may favor direct mail while major donors may want a special event or telephone call from the president. A media-habits survey can reveal not only that prospective students listen to radio but which radio format they listen to most often.

Questions you should ask relating to promotion:

■ To what media (TV, radio, advertising, direct mail) are our audiences most likely to respond?

■ What media are available in our target regions?

■ How do our promotional activities compare to those used by our competition?

■ What media can give us an edge?

Table 3-3.
Promotion Options

Word of mouth

Telemarketing

Signage and environmentals

Magazine advertising

Newspaper advertising

TV/cable advertising

Radio advertising

Transit/outdoor advertising

Multimedia (audio, video, floppies, CDs, Internet)

PSAs

Special events

Direct mail

Other Ps

The traditional definition of marketing focuses on price, product, place, and promotion. It is upon these that most marketing strategies are built. Of late, however, there has been much discussion about enlarging the four Ps to include three more concepts: policy, people, and performance.

Marketing as policy

You can evaluate the policy dimension by asking a simple question: Does this institution's policy-making body embrace marketing? Does it evaluate the marketing implications of policy decisions before making them? Is it willing to address or readdress policies that hinder marketing?

Marketing cannot thrive at institutions that do not understand how policy affects marketing. If the president wants to meet the needs of current students but refuses to allocate money to keep the financial aid office open during lunch hour, then marketing has failed at the policy level.

If the president's five-year plan emphasizes an increased commitment to alumni but refuses to allocate time or money to organize alumni events, marketing has failed at the policy level.

If the president charges a marketing task force with creating a plan but refuses to fund it, marketing has failed at the policy level. The policy dimension of marketing is critical. It is here that marketing will most likely succeed or fail. It is here that marketing moves from an idea to practice. It is here that marketing is sustained.

Marketing as people

The next P—people—reminds us that people define the marketing goals. People write the plan. People implement the plan. And people are the target of marketing strategies. Ultimately, the success of marketing relies on people.

People involved in marketing must be willing to be changed by the marketing process, to look at old things in new ways, to modify their actions, and to take responsibility for their efforts. In short, they must be committed to marketing.

This commitment will come neither easily nor quickly. A commitment cannot be mandated. Rather, it must be grown. A president once told me ruefully, "I don't worry about how my people do their jobs when I'm there. But I worry a lot about how they do their jobs when I am not."

Marketing as performance

The final P, marketing as performance, is an extension of marketing as people. Marketing as performance understands that the performance of people is what lifts marketing from plan to reality. People's commitment must be evident in their performance.

Barriers to marketing

Of course, the question must be asked: If the potential for marketing is so enormous, why do so few colleges and universities embrace it? This is a question I often ask at professional meetings and when I visit campuses. More often than not, the lament I hear follows this theme: "We don't have enough money."

In my experience, however, a lack of money is almost never the chief impediment to the creation and implementation of a comprehensive marketing strategy. Rather, the money issue usually masks other, often more entrenched, barriers. When I probe, I generally find one or more of the following systemic obstacles to marketing:

■ Prime motivators are missing. If stakeholders do not feel threatened, or if the

> "Ultimately, the success of marketing relies on people."

institution does not need the resources offered by emerging opportunities, it is unlikely that there will be enough consensus for marketing.

■ No top-down commitment to marketing. If the president doesn't aggressively support marketing, it will fail.

■ An ill-conceived belief that strategic problems can be solved tactically. All the direct mail in the world won't save a flawed, dated, or moribund curriculum.

■ An unwillingness to address issues of territoriality. Comprehensive marketing efforts are just that—comprehensive. If the chief academic, advancement, student services, and enrollment officers are not willing to share goals and resources, then the marketing effort will be seriously impaired.

■ A reluctance to undertake a realistic situational analysis. Marketing decisions must be founded on reliable information. A legitimate environmental audit, assessment of educational need, institutional self-study, and perception and positioning studies must be undertaken.

■ An inconsistent definition of marketing among senior administrators, plan developers, or other stakeholders. From the outset, planners and the campus community must use a common definition of marketing.

■ A confusion between stakeholders and customers. Stakeholders—faculty, staff, administrators, and others—are people who work for and support the institution. Customers are the people who pay the bills (donors actually have their feet in both camps). It is the job of the organization to serve its customers, and by meeting customer needs, it will gather resources that will support the needs of the stakeholders as well. However, if the institution is preoccupied with keeping stakeholders happy, it is likely that the needs and interests of the customer will be either ignored or shortchanged.

■ A fixation with historical paradigms. Colleges and universities exist in a society that is changing at a mind-boggling pace. As a consequence, institutions will find that traditions, self-perceptions, and historical patterns and ways of doing things are increasingly out of date, ill-suited, or overly costly. Consider the breadth of answers that the following questions might foster:
  • How do we define institutional success?
  • What is academic quality?
  • What students should we serve?
  • How do we define student success?

If your institution has not recently sought the answers to these questions, chances are it is out of touch with today's marketplace.

When I think about paradigm shifts and organizations and institutional resistance to change, I am reminded of the formula outlined below:

Number of years in current system x Age = Resistance to Change

In many respects, the people with the greatest stake in the status quo—senior administrators and faculty—are the same people who are in the best position to effect change. At the same time, the people most interested in change are often new entrants into the system and lack experience, power, or both. As a result, the potential for conflictual relationships will increase.

Characteristics of a market-oriented institution

While it is useful to spend some time describing institutional barriers to marketing, it is also important to outline the characteristics of a market-oriented institution, an institution that has the best opportunity to meet the challenges of an increasingly tempestuous marketing environment. The characteristics of these institutions include these:

- Embracing a comprehensive definition of marketing
- Recognizing marketplace dynamics
- A belief in the constancy of change
- Transforming vision
- Primacy of the customer
- Clarification of stakeholder roles
- Redefinition of quality and success
- A culture of "now!"
- Data-based decision-making
- Variation of product, price, place, and promotion
- Clear criteria for evaluating progress

Embracing a comprehensive definition of marketing

At the outset, market-oriented institutions embrace a comprehensive definition of marketing that clearly sets them apart from their peers. Rather than stressing only promotion, market-oriented institutions understand the need to develop strategic responses (produce, price, and place) to audience and marketplace needs and expectations and to communicate these strategic responses tactically, through aggressive promotion.

These few words address the fundamental difference between the growing handful of colleges and universities that are truly market-driven—that employ "integrated marketing" techniques—and the many that are not.

Recognizing marketplace dynamics

The second pivotal characteristic of a market-oriented institution is recognizing that the marketplace is dynamic, competitive, fluctuating, and, as one administrator reminded me, forgetful. We have learned from hard experience that the marketplace does not care about past successes. It does not care about traditions and accepted practices. It has its own definitions of academic quality. It does not guarantee you a certain share just because you exist. And perhaps most important for this discussion, the marketplace has too few students to fill the classrooms and too few donors to fill the coffers of today's colleges and universities.

This is the marketplace in which you must compete for students and donated dollars.

A belief in the constancy of change

Market-oriented institutions also understand that the only real constant in today's marketing environment is change and that in response to this changing environment, colleges and universities must be willing to change as well.

Change is difficult in any organization, but it is perhaps more so in higher education where tradition is so treasured. Recently, a colleague passed on a wonderful illustration that outlined the steps for managing change in complex systems (see Figure 3-2). That illustration noted that enabling change requires five key ingredients:

- Vision
- Skills
- Incentives
- Resources
- Action plans

Vision provides badly needed direction. Skills, both technical and human, are used to execute strategy. Incentives are designed to encourage and to soften discord. Resources pay for the execution of strategies. And action plans, a clear sense of who is doing what, are meant to provide accountability. These are the ingredients of change, and if one or more is missing, change either will not occur or will likely not be long-term.

Transforming vision

The next characteristic of a market-oriented institution, as noted in Chapter 2, is transforming vision.

Primacy of the customer

Market-oriented institutions understand the primacy of their customers. They know their demographic and psychographic profiles. They know their needs and expectations. They know where and how they live. They know their motivations, fears, and

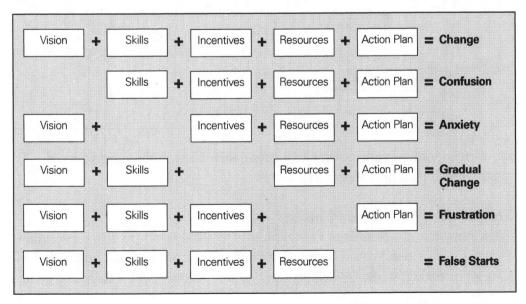

Figure 3-2
Managing Change
Source: *Unknown*

concerns. And perhaps most important, they never, ever forget that it is the customers who pay the bills.

Understanding and accepting the primacy of the customer should affect organizational structure in a significant way. Regis McKenna, writing in *Relationship Marketing: Successful Strategies for the Age of the Customer*, presents the notion of a director or vice president of "market relations" rather than marketing. The application of this thinking to higher education might lead to an organizational structure that resembles the chart in Figure 3-3.

In this organizational model, one senior administrator, the vice president for market relations, oversees all customer relations regardless of the stage at which that customer relates to the institution. Clearly, this structure is pushing the organizational envelope.

Clarification of stakeholder roles

Market-oriented institutions fully understand the important contribution that stakeholders—faculty, staff, and other constituents—make to academic quality and the totality of the educational experience. They also understand, however, that although stakeholder voices should never be overlooked, theirs are not the only voices. Institutions should continue to acknowledge stakeholders' important role, but mar-

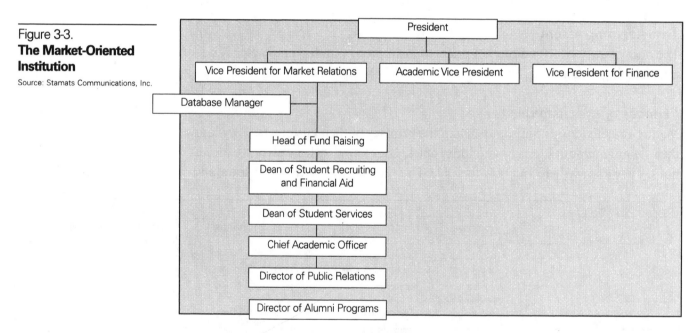

Figure 3-3.
The Market-Oriented Institution

Source: Stamats Communications, Inc.

ket-oriented institutions know that to focus on their needs at the expense of customers is to imperil the entire enterprise.

Redefinition of quality and success

Often in my role as a consultant I ask administrators and faculty to define institutional quality and success. When I began asking this question 10 years ago, quality and success centered on students—helping them achieve academically, socially, and even spiritually. Over the past couple of years, however, definitions of quality and success have begun to emphasize financial stability (cash flow, endowment, fund raising, new sources of revenue) and building programs (I often jokingly term this preoccupation with facilities the "edifice complex"). Somehow, students are being squeezed out.

Market-oriented institutions need to rediscover, or perhaps just emphasize anew, student-centered definitions of quality and success. Though accounting ledgers should balance, facilities should shine, and endowments should grow, it must be recognized that these are all means to a larger end of educating and enriching students. They are not ends unto themselves.

A culture of "now!"

Colleges and universities need a keen sense of now. They need to understand that opportunities are fleeting. They need to deliberate more quickly. And they need to act decisively. They need to develop a culture of "now!"

I believe that a culture of "now!" has seven characteristics. First, there is an empowering sense of entrepreneurship. Causes and ideas are encouraged. People are on teams rather than committees. Champions step forward. Leaders have followers. Things happen—some great, some not so great, and many unexpected.

Second, risk-taking is encouraged. It is a commitment to the status quo, not failure, that is discouraged. Third, there is an attitude of immediacy. Deliberation and debate are still valued, but undue deliberation and debate are not. Talk, but talk quickly.

Fourth, institutions with a culture of "now!" understand that they cannot afford perfect decisions. They realize that they have neither the time nor the money to assess and consider every contingency. The goal should not be perfect decisions but a string of pretty good decisions made in a timely fashion. Market-oriented institutions understand that their future does not lie along a straight path. Rather, their future is a series of zigs and zags—missteps and corrections toward a generalized goal.

Fifth, while consensus is valued when it occurs, it is not expected, and when it doesn't occur, the institution still moves forward. Institutions with a culture of "now!" recognize that there will be disagreements, even conflict. Some people and departments will have their horizons expanded, and others will find theirs eclipsed. Market-oriented institutions make no guarantees that individuals will be happy and secure. In fact, this is not a goal. Enhancing the institution's ability to meet the needs of its customers is.

Sixth, there is much more interest in fixing problems than in affixing blame. On too many campuses, blame slides downhill, with senior administrators blaming junior administrators and everyone blaming the faculty. Colleges and universities cannot afford this preoccupation with blame. Acknowledge your mistakes. Assess the mechanisms that failed. Make adjustments or corrections. And move on.

Finally, colleges and universities with a culture of "now!" have a strong sense of individual and group accountability. Accountability is a given.

> **Market-oriented institutions understand that their future does not lie along a straight path.**

Data-based decision-making

The next characteristic of a market-oriented institution is a data-based approach to decision-making. Solid, defensible data will be aggressively sought, considered for a prescribed time, and acted on. Peppers and Rogers in *Enterprise One to One: Tools for Competing in the Interactive Age* introduce a wonderful term: the learning relationship. The learning relationship describes an intimate interaction between the organization and its customers. It is a relationship built on trust, on aggressive listening by the organization, and on two-way communication (not merely promotion). At all times, this relationship recognizes and meets the self-interests of both parties—the organization and the customer.

Interestingly, the desire for a learning relationship presents us with an odd conundrum. For organizations to be highly personal, they must rely on impersonal data, a perfect record of all interactions between the organization and the customer. Generally, the ability to create and maintain perfect records is not a technology issue or even a cost issue but more an issue of institutional will and intent. Making data-based decisions may hinder the freewheeling or recalcitrant style of some administrators or faculty.

Even as we develop and refine our data collection and data-based decision-making abilities, we would do well to remember the Laws of Data Dynamics. While data are important, and more data are generally more insightful than fewer data, there are some basic cautions to keep in mind. See Table 3-4.

Variation of product, price, place, and promotion

Market-oriented institutions do not treat all customers to the same product, price, place, and promotion. There is a willingness to customize and segment. There is a willingness to modify and test. And there is a willingness to treat some customers differently than others on the basis of their ability to return value—dollars, ability, or some quality or characteristic that the institution desires.

In some respects, the willingness of the institution to customize product, price, place, and promotion strategies is a logical extension of two key issues: its desire to embrace a more comprehensive definition of marketing and its willingness to act on data.

Clear criteria for evaluating progress

Clear criteria are the final characteristic of a market-oriented institution. Ideally, these criteria are established *a priori* rather than *ex post facto*. Perhaps the greatest difference between business and education is the historic reluctance of colleges and universities to evaluate systematically whether programs, strategies, activities, and plans make sense, whether they are effective, and whether they are contributing value. There is a feeling, a strong one, that business-based measures of success and progress simply have nothing to offer higher education. For market-oriented institutions, this is no longer true.

Recently I had an opportunity to speak to an administrator from a League of

---

Table 3-4.
Laws of Data Dynamics

- People misinterpret.
- Data are seldom as accurate as people say.
- Data age quickly.
- Data will always be used for purposes other than that for which they were originally gathered.
- Data collected about individuals will be used to cause inconvenience to members of the group that provided the information or about which it was collected.
- Confidential information is confidential only until someone decides it's not.
- Data migrate.

Modified from Larson's *The Naked Consumer*

Innovation community college. She noted that her institution sets clear goals before launching new programs. If a program does not meet these goals, it is cut or reconfigured. This must be the model for all of higher education in the future, just as it is the model for marketing.

4

Market Research

A foundation built on research

Solid marketing plans rest on a foundation of research. In fact, any marketing plan that does not include research at its base is almost surely flawed. It either will fail or will take more time and money to execute. This reality is reflected in a basic definition of market research: the systematic design, collection, analysis, and reporting of data and findings relevant to a specific marketing situation an institution faces. In short, market research involves finding specific answers to specific questions—information that is used to refine marketing goals and to help develop the overall marketing plan.

Market research can help you in a variety of ways. First, you can use it to gather perceptual data. Because people act on their perceptions, learning how different audiences perceive and sometimes misperceive you is critical.

Second, you can use research to provide answers. A recent client was interested in knowing which of two academic programs would attract the most students. A survey of prospective students, an analysis of competing curricula, and an evaluation of short- and long-term regional job and employment trends provided the necessary data. Another client wanted to know which message strategies prospective donors might best respond to. A survey of donors quickly pinpointed some strategies the client had not previously considered.

Third, research helps you clarify and set priorities. In today's marketing, fund-raising, and recruiting environment, the problem is generally not a lack of options but determining which ones are most likely to succeed or provide the greatest return in the shortest time. If you have $10,000 to buy advertising aimed at nontraditional students, you can use research to pinpoint the media to which they are most likely to respond.

Fourth, research allows you to test ideas. With research, you can evaluate publication concepts, logo ideas, even signage. Using research in this way can often prevent you from making expensive and very public mistakes.

And finally, research helps monitor your environment. It can quickly pinpoint problems while they are still manageable. At the same time, research can highlight opportunities that you might otherwise miss.

Not data but information

It is not difficult to generate research data. Chances are you have volumes of data sitting on a shelf somewhere in your office. Rather than just data, successful research must generate information upon which you can act. In other words, it is not the collection of data that matters most but the interpretation and application of data.

Each year, college administrators send my company multivolumed studies done by nationally known research companies. Accompanying the studies is a question: "What did we learn—would you mind going over the numbers for us and letting us know what we found out?"

Good research, research that can be used to support a marketing plan, must do more than gather data. It must provide answers to real questions. It must provide clear direction. And it must set out options in priority order.

A necessary vocabulary

Like any specialized endeavor, market research has its own vocabulary. It is important to understand some key terms before we begin a more detailed discussion.

Primary research and secondary research

Essentially, there are two sources of research data: primary and secondary. Primary research uses data that originate with your specific study. Secondary research uses existing data from a completed study that may be applicable to yours.

Suppose, for example, you want to know why alumni give to your institution. If you conduct a survey to find out, you are engaged in primary research. On the other hand, if you use data from a study completed by a colleague at another institution, you are using secondary research.

The difference is important for several reasons. First, because primary research involves designing an original study, it is more expensive and time-consuming. Secondary research is usually less expensive or even free and is usually available quickly.

The second major difference involves the quality, suitability, and integrity of the

> **"Good research must do more than gather data."**